LAINI NASH

My Christian Walk

TABLE OF CONTENTS

I'll take a stand	7
I take delight	8
I won't be beat	9
Your light	11
I try	12
The right partner	13
Why Lord	14
When things go wrong	15
Animals	16
Holy, Holy, Holy is the Lord	17
Questions for God	18
Why not suicide	21
A simple poem	22
Just thankful	23
Just a word	24
A message from Heaven	25
Faith not luck	26
Angels	27

Hallelujah to the Lord	28
Please come Lord	29
Lord why?	31
My day	32
What's important	33
A beautiful life	34
Do you always love me?	35
My choice	36
Bringing up children	38
Hurting world	39
A Christian walk	41
God is…	42
God works for me	43
God is always around	44
Thank you my God	45
Sunday school	46
You amaze me Lord	47
Antichrist	48
Hallelujah	49
Searching	51

You're there for me	52
I saw Heaven	53
A gift	54
Peace	55
Non-believer	56
A poem of praise	57
The good things	58
Mom said I should	59
A better world	60
My poems	61
Dixie	62
Love blankets	63
Starting over	64
For the Queen on Prince Phillip's passing	65
I've seen	66
You are my sunshine	67
A simple poem	68
Just thankful	69
I stray	70
My body is sick	71

A song on my lips	72
I feel for those who don't know	73
Can we talk	74
Little creatures	75
God's way	76
Take me	77
Anew	78
Girl of my past	79

I'LL TAKE A STAND

Today I'll do the right thing, I'll stand tall,
I know you'll help see me through it all.
Though it's harder to do the right thing,
I'll show my heart and let my soul sing.
My foots on the rock, my faith in God alone,
it's because of the love God has shone.
Today I'll beat sin where normally I fall,
God loves me so I will give him my all.
Yeah it's easier to sin then repent,
this is not a life well spent.
So dear Father, take me by the hand,
I'll do the right thing; I'll take a stand.

I TAKE DELIGHT

Dear God, I'll never stop taking delight in you,
from the lessons you teach to the miracles you do.
I'm happy with lessons even when I'm wrong,
I want to sing your praises in a beautiful song.
I adore all the wonderful gifts you give,
I seek to please you with the way I live.
Thank you for the Bible that left your instruction,
the best day of my life was your introduction.
I'm in awe of the way you work your deeds,
how you lovingly provide for all our needs.
Dear God, I take such delight in you,
I want to help others to know you too.

I WON'T BE BEAT

I will not drown in shallow water,
my faith in God will not falter.
I will beat sin the best I know,
I'll do this to let God's love show.
I will not fall before my enemies on the ground,
through my actions I'll show God can be found
The food I eat will not have poison within,
for with God, over evil I will win.
I'll swim the ocean with no land in sight,
there's a Heavenly current I will not fight.
I won't be beat, I'll walk in grace,
I have faith one day I'll see your face.

YOUR LIGHT

God I see, I see your light,
never let it disappear from my sight.
The only way I can change the world we're in,
is to encourage others to turn from sin.
I can share your word and all you do,
so others get to know you too.
Maybe if others know how we should live,
more tolerance and compassion they would give
Your commandments aren't hard
they're meant for our good,
to teach us to love and live the way we should.
Try not to hurt or look for personal gain,
help peace and love in our world to remain.
There's so much good in shinning your light,
if we practice love we'll be alright.

I TRY

I pray for my enemies and I forgive,
if I don't, how can I expect you to give.
I'm not popular when I do the right thing,
but I know doing this peace it will bring.
I'm no goody goody, I'm not perfect it's true,
I just do my best to serve and please you.
My feelings get hurt, I cry sometimes too,
but I try to submit in all I do.
I give you my problems, I know that's okay,
I know your love will see me through the day.
So Lord, see my heart when you look at me,
know I'm trying to be the best I can be.

THE RIGHT PARTNER

Lord, how do I find the right partner for me?
I know you'll bring the one so I wait patiently.
I'm in no rush, I want it to be right,
able to be blessed in your sight.
A partner with whom my love I can share,
as intended by you, one who'll always be there.
More than physical, it's a deeper love,
like the kind you give from Heaven above.
So Lord, when I'm ready please bring the one to me
like the Bible says we'll be yoked equally.

WHY LORD

Lord there's one thing that shakes people's faith
and makes them cry,
this happens when our loved ones die.
Why must it happen, why must it be,
I want to keep my loved ones with me.
Lord one thing more makes us turn away,
it's the evil and badness we see each day.
You're the one blamed for the pain we're in,
in know it's not you, it's people who sin.
you gave freedom of choice, you didn't take that away,
only for now the devil has his day.
You will come back, the pain will cease,
those who follow will find peace.

WHEN THINGS GO WRONG

When things go wrong as they sometimes do,
I know Lord, all i need is you.
When the road ahead seems all up hill,
I stop and wonder if this is your will.
I know better than to blame it on you,
you don't control what people do.
You live where you're accepted,
this relationship is protected.
Bad things will happen, that's how the world is,
things won't change until in Heaven we live.
So Lord, I thank you most humbly,
for the good things you give to me.

ANIMALS

why can't a skunk be not smelly and bite,
why can't I pet a tiger without a cat fight?
Why can't a monkey be handled without the monkeying around,
I just want to be friends with all the animals I have found.
Just to care for, cuddle, pet and play,
I like to meet a new one each day.
God you made them wonderful but a bit dangerous too,
I bet they don't act this way with you.
So I'll wait to see them in Heaven one day,
where together we will roam and play.

HOLY, HOLY, HOLY IS THE LORD

The song in my heart sings to the Lord,
I want him to know he's adored,
Holy, Holy, Holy is the Lord.
I sing to you the best I can,
I want everyone to understand,
Holy, Holy, Holy is the Lord.
When things go wrong, I pray to you,
the Lord is good this is true,
Holy, Holy, Holy is the Lord.
When I walk down a road unpaved,
I'm loved all because God gave,
Holy, Holy, Holy is the Lord.
When I am lonely, feeling depressed,
the Lord has always given his best,
Holy, Holy, Holy is the Lord,
Holy is the Lord.

QUESTIONS FOR GOD

I have a few questions for God you see,
things that just don't make sense to me.
Like why do innocent babies die?
It breaks our heart and makes us cry.

Why do bad things happen
to good people we know?
Why must it hurt so for us to grow?
Why is there so much evil around,
please tell me where the answers can be found.

Will I really see my loved ones
who've passed away,
here is what the Heavenly spirit had to say…
My child I can't tell you all of my plan,
but evils been around since time began.

As for the innocent I now have here with me,
I have reasons that one day you'll see.
There's freedom of choice I've given to you,
that is why people do what they do.

And as for your loved ones, believers will see,
you'll reunite one day in Heaven with me.
As for love it's a good thought and a prayer,
turn to me I will always be there.

Keep your faith, stay close to me,
do your best is what I ask of thee,
then one day my plan you'll see.

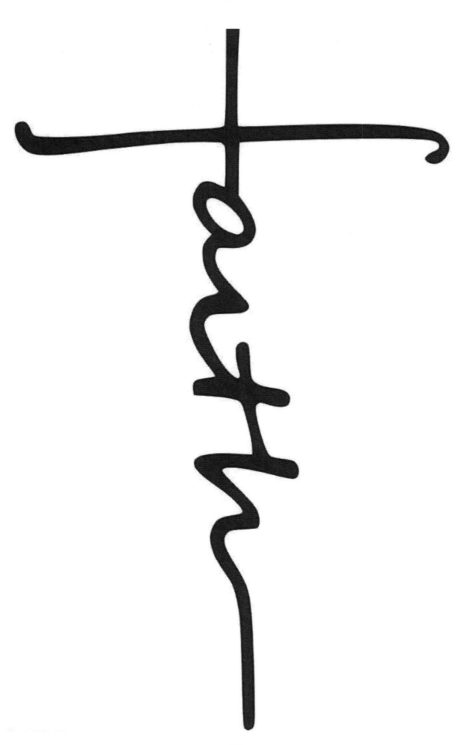

WHY NOT SUICIDE

I'm tired of the earth where I roam,
I want to go to Heaven where I call home.
I'm tired of the games people play,
it's an evil world where I don't want to stay.
I stay because you have a purpose for me,
though what it is presently I can't see.
I follow your plan the best I know,
even though I really want to go.
To love someone is to keep them in prayer,
I know life won't always be fair.
I love regardless and pray every day,
until you decide, here I will stay.

A SIMPLE POEM

A Bible verse a day,
scares the devil away.
A daily prayer to Heaven,
keeps you in touch brethren.
Faith today helps tomorrow grow,
it's all about love don't you know.
The choice is yours it's very clear,
tomorrow may be too late for a tear.

JUST THANKFUL

I have thanks in my heart, you on my mind,
for all the love and peace you helped me find.
There's so much I'd have missed if I didn't let you in.
I'd still be lost, unhappy, bound by sin.
I've learned the lessons you had to teach,
you've brought my goals within my reach.
I'll never cease thanking you,
it's what my soul wants to do.
So thank you Lord for being with me,
and opening my eyes so I can see.

JUST A WORD

Oh Lord! My burdens seem heavy today,
it seems my problems won't go away.
I confess I don't know what to do,
I'm too depressed to even pray to you,
then the Holy spirit comes to me,
and says don't worry the Lord can see.
Just a few words, the prayer need not belong,
God is lovingly willing to fix what is wrong.
Lord please fix things, I can't talk right now,
I don't know what to say, I don't know how.
I stare into space then my phone rings,
I'm encouraged by the good news it brings.
I found money in my jeans I'd forgotten,
suddenly my day doesn't seem so rotten,
I send up a short word of praise,
thank you for being in all of my days.

A MESSAGE FROM HEAVEN

I asked for an angel with a message from you,
I asked for many days not just one or two.
Finally a morning dove came into view,
I knew it's presence was a message from you.
The morning dove is a message of praise, faith and love
such a wonderful message from Heaven above.
Thank you for answering my prayer for me,
your answer came in a form I could see.

FAITH NOT LUCK

I knew I could do it, I did it through you,
through God, there's nothing i can't do.
The Bible makes all these promises you see,
I believe them all deep inside of me.
Nothing happens through luck alone,
you understand when in faith you've grown.
Nothing happens by your own hands,
it happens through God, please understand.
Yes things happen by choices you make,
God gave us free will, not by mistake.
It's by this free will you walk in grace,
it's by faith you live and will see God's face.

ANGELS

The wings of Angels spread far and wide,
their love for God they don't hide.
Do they light up or wear a halo on their head,
do they come from the living or the dead?
Do they eat, sleep, run or play,
do they do miracles or just suggest a way,
how will they prove they're an Angel to me,
are they invisible or something I can see?
I'm curious about Angels and all they do,
has an Angel ever come to visit you?

HALLELUJAH TO THE LORD

I sing to you oh Lord,
hallelujah to the Lord.
You love and provide for me,
God is good, the Holy spirit visits me.
I sing to you oh Lord,
hallelujah to the Lord.
My comforter, my strength, a friend to me,
you love me so completely.
Hallelujah I sing to the Lord.
Hallelujah to the Lord.
Always caring, always guiding,
a love always abiding.
Hallelujah, hallelujah,
I sing to you oh Lord,
hallelujah to the Lord.

PLEASE COME LORD

Lord, why don't you stop the bad people do,
isn't this world up to you?
I know with the devil is where evil starts,
he's destroying the world, tearing us apart.
He causes death, pain, turmoil and trauma,
he fills the world with his terrible drama.
When will you come to save us all,
and cause the devil to permanently fall?

LORD WHY?

Lord do you see what's happening
from Heaven on high,
do you see our pain or hear when we cry?
When we get hurt do you understand?
are we healed by the works of your hand?
When we are sad, are you sad too,
do you give us a happier point of view?
When we're crushed by the world and all its deeds,
when we have nothing do you provide for our needs
Lord, why must we wait for a time unknown,
to see you sitting on your throne.

MY DAY

Good morning Lord, I start this way,
thank you for yet another day.
Bless my day and the people I love,
keep your hand on me from Heaven above.
Help me meet the challenges I face,
and any problems in this rat race.
Help me remember to let your love show,
to others as they come and go.
Keep me close within your favor,
bless my work as I labor.
Let me know you've heard the words I said,
keep me happy as I go to bed.

WHAT'S IMPORTANT

Lord, I know it's important to listen to you,
to seek you first in all I do.
It's important that I let your love show,
The Holy spirit is with me wherever I go.
I try to be understanding in angers place,
to be forgiving and pass on your grace.
I won't have sex until i marry a man,
I give to my neighbor a helping hand.
You are important, so are your ways,
I try to display this as I live out my days.

A BEAUTIFUL LIFE

Such a beautiful life you've given me,
home, a purpose, a family.
Though it's not always easy I'm grateful to thee,
I know in all I do you walk beside me.
I have so many choices of things to do,
choices and free will given by you.
You provide for me and you protect me,
I'm blessed it's easy to see.
Lord, I love you I praise you,
with my whole heart this I do.
Thank you Lord for loving me so,
you are with me and love me wherever I go.

DO YOU ALWAYS LOVE ME?

Lord, I can't explain the mood I'm in,
if I'm mad at you is it a sin?
I asked you for something important to me,
I watched and waited but no answer I see.
Sometimes I just want things my way,
is that really so horrible to say.
I know I should pray your will not mine,
I'm just not obedient all of the time.
Do you still love me when I get this way?
I get afraid you will walk away.
Lord help me remember you have a plan,
when confused, help me to understand.
I know that you love me in all that I do,
despite these moments, I Love you too.

MY CHOICE

Dear God my parents taught me of you,
to love you is what I want to do.
You can lead a horse to water, but can't make him drink,
they told me of you but not what to think.

No matter your background you think for yourself one day,
it was my choice to stay close, my choice to pray.
I'm thankful they introduced you or I'd have no chance at all,
I'm thankful I answered when I heard your call.

You see Lord it's by choice I stay close to you,
and try to inject you in all that I do.
I know you give the choice to be or not be,
but to stay close to you is the choice for me.

Some children grow up never hearing of you,
some parents don't know the right thing to do.

We need churches and people to speak of you often,
so your legacy of love is never forgotten.

How can we make a choice if we don't know the menu
this is why for children, church is a good venue.
So I made my choice, it's perfectly clear,
children must be told of you from their first year.

BRINGING UP CHILDREN

We have a duty to children to bring them up well,
that's why it's important of God to tell.
We must teach by words and actions too,
don't you think children watch what you do?
We must teach them and let them choose,
to be informed, we must tell them the news.
So hear my advice, bring your children up right,
teach them to turn from the dark to the light.

HURTING WORLD

Lord what's going on in the world is painful to see
but Revelations says it's the way it must be.
Your precious animals are being hurt and abused,
by the Evil one people are used.
Affordable housing, Lord there isn't enough,
our once safe streets have become really rough.
Our children are hungry, without any food,
too much stress puts us all in a bad mood.
There are more fires, quakes and hurricanes too,
they destroy the earth with what they do.
Bad crimes are up it's horrible to see,
but Revelations says it's how it must be.
I believe the end times are what we're in,
but we have your promise the Devil won't win.

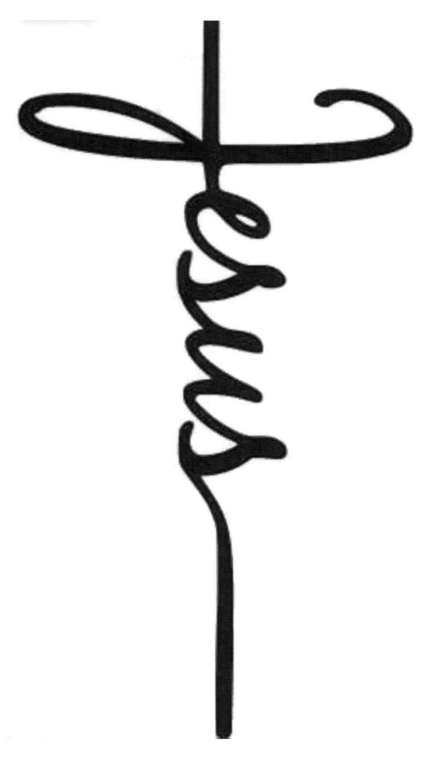

A CHRISTIAN WALK

God, could we have a serious talk?
It's about a true Christian walk.
Some Christians they talk a good game,
while secretly living a life of shame.
They criticize others for not doing good,
while they don't live the way they should.
They talk of God, they are quite a bore,
problems of their own they ignore.
When is the last time they gave of their time?
Or honestly prayed "Lord you're will not mine."
they only act like Christians they should be,
only doing good for the world to see.
Sure they put money in the collection plate,
but what they preach and do don't equate.
When is the last time they cleaned house for someone
When without them it couldn't get done.
There are so many things a Christian could do,
especially if they are truly serving you.

GOD IS...

God is my Father, there is no other,

this makes the world my brother.

We don't treat everyone like family,

forgetting what we should and shouldn't be.

We should treat everyone important and with love,

pleasing our Father in Heaven above.

God is my friend so close and so dear,

it is to Him, I try to draw near.

I try to abide by his rules and laws,

I work daily to remove my flaws.

God is my light, he is all that I need,

to him daily I concede.

GOD WORKS FOR ME

God is a caring, loving Heavenly Father,
I confess with churches I don't bother.
Churches break into religions don't you see,
I stick to my Bible so they don't confuse me.
My Heavenly father provides for me well,
He gives me so much, of all it's hard to tell.
God listens and responds,
corrects me when I'm wrong,
this is why I lift my voice to praise Him in song.
God helps me when I'm lost,
forgives me when I've sinned,
when I have to start over He shows me where to begin
God provides all my needs in a caring way,
I'll love Him until eternity and a day.

GOD IS ALWAYS AROUND

God is a loving God, he'll never let you down,
no matter where you are he's always around.
Receiving the Holy spirit is like a pill you take,
it's a conscious decision you make.
Once you've received you must change inside,
of everything you do there's nothing you can hide.
You want to do better, obey God's laws,
God accepts you completely even with flaws.
If you ask, God will guide you and see you through,
he loves you always, no matter what you do.
You'll have the Holy spirit, that little voice inside,
it also helps you and guides you to abide.
God is a loving God, he'll never let you down,
no matter where you are he's always around.

THANK YOU MY GOD

My God, my God, is so good to me,
I want to tell all so all can see.
He loves me no matter what I do,
my God is wonderful and loves you too.
I'm comfortable and happy as can be,
this is because God provides all for me.
Thank you God, thank you indeed,
you are my one and only need.

SUNDAY SCHOOL

Sunday school is the place to be,
whether for the young or old like me.
You hear stories from the Bible, tried and true,
to know these stories is good for you.
You should read more than a story,
always give God the glory.
There are important words and phrases too,
the Bible tells us what we should do.
Sunday school is a wonderful place to be,
come on friend, read the Bible with me.

YOU AMAZE ME LORD

I had no food, in my wallet 50 cents did I see,
then a random check came in the mail to me.
Lord, I don't know how you do it you're so good,
you love me eve when I don't do what I should.
My every need you know and provide for me,
because you're in my life I'm blessed as can be.
I mean, I didn't know I was that precious to you,
but it shows every day in all that you do.
Thank you Lord for knowing and loving me so,
I love you too just so you know.

ANTICHRIST

A pastor, the devil in disguise,
pushing "miracle water", these are lies.
Getting rich with words they say,
words I didn't find in the bible today.
Watch who you follow, what they do,
Satan is waiting to mislead you.

HALLELUJAH

Hallelujah my Savior lives,
it's a perfect love he gives.
You always come with perfect love,
you bring your grace from above.
Hallelujah my Savior lives,
it's a perfect love that he gives.
I want you here in my life to stay,
I need you so every day.
I fall and you come to me,
you lift me up so I can see.
Hallelujah my Savior lives,
it's a perfect love he gives.
Hallelujah thank you Lord,
Hallelujah praise the Lord.

SEARCHING

Dear God I'm searching for you,
please tell me what I need to do.
Do I need faith in what I can't see?
Do you see the desire inside of me?
How do I love those I hate?
Please tell me now before it's too late.
I give to those less fortunate that me,
I give out of love most happily.
Do I really need to go to church, is that really true
Why do I need a building to glorify you?
God I'm searching, searching for you,
please be beside me in all that I do.

YOU'RE THERE FOR ME

You lift me up when I am down,
you help turn my life around.
Your perfect love is precious to me,
I tell the world so all can see.
I dream at night in peaceful slumber,
you love me so it's no wonder.
I reach for you with a heart so true,
willing to do what you ask me to.
When I awake and meet the day,
I can't start until I pray.
Then I rise and get out of bed,
thoughts of you fill my head.
Bless this day I'm about to face,
cover me with your love and grace.

I SAW HEAVEN

Dear God last night I dreamed of Heaven above
I felt the immenseness of your love.
I had an angel voice and angel wings,
I had no need for material things.
When I awoke all I could do was sigh,
at least for now I had to say goodbye.
I won't forget all that I saw,
I got pencil and paper and began to draw.
I couldn't come close to all I had seen
I guess beauty like that only lives in a dream.
Heaven is a dream I will see again one day,
this is my hope, for this I pray.

A GIFT

God you always answer my every prayer,
I never doubt that you are there.
I don't know why I'm so special to you,
but you make that clear in all you do.
You protect me when I don't even know,
when danger doesn't always show.
You love me when loveable I don't always feel,
when I'm sick you're the one who heals.
When I sin or lose my way,
you let me start over every day.
When I break a commandment or hurt you with sin,
your forgiveness is complete it's nothing I have to win.
When I'm so sad I want to go away,
you put something before me to brighten my day.
Oh dear Lord how do I thank you for all you do?
All I have is my heart pure and true.
So God please accept my gist and always stay,
I need and love you every day.

PEACE

No matter your religion or your view,
Peace has to begin with you.
Keep your feelings and opinions but you will find,
you can do this while practicing love leave hate behind.
See, life is hard enough for each of us each day,
without engaging in the means, hurtful games people play.
God made us each to have compassion and love,
He made us in God's image from heaven above.
Yes, it is scary to trust and can hurt to forgive,
but the way we're living is no way to live.
Don't take from others we must live as a whole,
no money, drugs, hurt feelings is worth your soul.
So live with each other, love every day,
this is the only way peace will stay.

NON-BELIEVER

You say you don't believe in God, let me tell you this,
not believing, there is so much you will miss.
Just because there is bad doesn't mean He's not there,
He gives you what you need not want just because He cares.
He's not a magic genie to make a wish come true,
but He will always love you, no matter what you do.
Believe or not He loves you just the same,
you only need to ask for help, just call out His name.
God has grace and forgiveness waiting there for you,
to accept and trust Him is all you need to do.
He wants your love, He's waiting, so what will you do?
I'm telling you He won't force you the choice is up to you
He is there though you can't see His face,
I promise in the end, you will want His grace.
So just try, you have nothing to lose,
God loves you, this is the good news.

A POEM OF PRAISE

Heavenly Father, this is a poem of praise,
I am thankful you are in all of my days.
I have needs I don't even ask for,
yet you let your blessings pour.
You give my needs and wants too,
my best is all you ask me to do.
Thank you Lord for all you do for me,
your works in my life are very plain to see.
Thank you Lord for loving me,
you make me all I can be.
Praise you Lord!

THE GOOD THINGS

The wind in my hair, grass beneath my feet,
living in the country just can't be beat.
The smell of hay a fresh apple off the tree,
plenty of room to roam, room to be free.
Vegetables from the garden, I raise my own meet,
chemical free food is such a treat.
I sit on the front porch swing at night,
heavenly stars not hidden by city lights.
In front of the fireplace I sip a brandy,
a new baby foal is quite dandy.
This the life, the life that I love,
I always give thanks to God above.

MOM SAID I SHOULD

My mother did the best she could,
so I would grow up the way I should.
It's true when it came to love she was cold,
but she knew in life I'd need to be bold.
She taught me of God and how to be good,
to stay close to God the way I should.
With her own body she protected my life,
from my dad, she was his wife.
I can't handle all the beatings I saw her take,
but she did it for me, for my own sake.
She taught me manners and to be kind,
all her lessons affected my mind.
She taught me the shoulds, then let me go,
I was ten it was my time to grow.
I thank and love you for all you went through,
you taught and told me the things I should do.
So, rest in peace all your work is done,
in this race called life, I've finally won.

A BETTER WORLD

If the world could be renewed for good,
and people lived the way they should.
The world a happy place would be,
it wouldn't seem so horrible to me.
Anger, hate and violence too,
would be things we use to do.
Understanding, compassion and love,
would be infused by God above.
The world would be a better place,
I would have a smile on my face.

MY POEMS

I write my poems from verses in my head,
I hope they get carefully read.
Each has a point I'm trying to make,
I write carefully not to make a mistake.
I hope people take my words to heart,
for peace, love and God, a place to start.
I make some very good points you see,
the words come from inside of me.
I want the world to hear the words I write,
so anger and hatred through love we fight.
So read my words and let them sink in,
for a better world, it's a place to begin.

DIXIE

Thank you Lord for a beautiful day,
but Lord, some don't feel that way.
I pray for their souls that are hurting,
remove the evil from which they're flirting.
Remove any bad or evil from their day,
come into their life to fully stay.
Their torment is real and most demanding,
They need your clarity and understanding.
They need your protection that much is clear,
please Lord help them, to them draw near.

LOVE BLANKETS

Lord, I make these gifts with my own two hands,
doubting sometimes the receiver understands.
It takes time and love to do what I do,
while making these blankets, I pray to you.
I crochet blankets for people I love,
while praying for blessings from Heaven above.
I want to make them happy and feel special too,
this is why I take time to do what I do.
You can't buy this blanket in a store you see,
this blanket was made with love by me.
These love blankets that I crochet,
are made just for them on which to lay.

STARTING OVER

I reach out my hand and ask what's wrong,
you say your life is gone.
Your husband cheated now your apart,
you can't fix it, you don't know where to start.
So there goes your home and family,
you can start over listen to me.
It starts with a prayer, a word to God,
just start talking it's not odd.
Don't put your faith in men, they'll let you down,
put your faith in God he's always around.
When you meet the right guy you will know,
don't forget to let God's light show.
So see life is good it will get better,
write in your heart God's love letter.

FOR THE QUEEN ON PHILLIP'S PASSING

When people die where do they go?
They go to heaven don't you know.
They are with our father in a kingdom so rare,
so take comfort he is in good care.
Not gone forever you will see him one day,
God's great love just works that way.
Prince Phillip will watch from Heaven above,
that a tribute to a great love.
So keep going, let the sun shine on your face,
I pray God comforts you with his grace.

I'VE SEEN

I've seen the beauty of the Isles,
I've seen peoples smiles.
I've seen the morning flower touched by dew,
I've seen the beauty inside of you.
I've seen the amazing birth of a child,
I've seen the frolic of animals in the wild.
I've played in the downpour of the rain,
I've done some things that seem insane.
There is so much beauty around,
in the sky, the water and on the ground.
If you look you'll be amazed,
beauty surrounds us in so many ways.

YOU ARE MY SUNSHINE

You are my sunshine, light of my life,
you keep me going when there is strife.
"I love you" can't explain how I feel,
it's a love so deep and so real.
You make me happy when I am sad,
you make me laugh when I am mad.
We are alone so I have to be,
giving in all you need of me.
You make my life more than it could be,
my sons you are precious to me.
Mom, dad, nurse, playmate and friend,
family is what matters in the end.
Being a single parent is hard you see,
I'm grateful God gave you to me.

A SIMPLE POEM

A Bible verse a day,
scares the devil away.
A daily prayer to Heaven,
keeps you in touch brethren.
Faith today helps tomorrow grow,
it's all about love don't you know.
The choice is yours it's very clear,
tomorrow may be too late for a tear.

JUST THANKFUL

I have thanks in my heart, you on my mind,
for all the love and peace you helped me find.
There's so much I'd have missed if I didn't let you in
I'd still be lost, unhappy, bound by sin.
I've learned the lessons you had to teach,
you've brought my goals within my reach.
I'll never cease thanking you,
it's what my soul wants to do.
So thank you Lord for being with me,
and opening my eyes so I can see.

I STRAY

Dear Lord, I'm grateful for all you give,
you always love me no matter how I live.
I sometimes forget to pray every day,
it's easier at times to go my own way.
I'm flawed and imperfect, a sinner it's true,
but you always forgive no matter what I do.
I'm blessed to have you in my life I know,
I try to let your good works show.
Dear Lord, I/m grateful for the love you give,
so I keep trying to improve the way I live.

MY BODY IS SICK

God my body is sick, my mind is weak,
in times of trouble, it's you I seek.
I did everything right yet things went wrong,
I need you Lord I'm not that strong.
I know I need not wonder where you are,
for you've always proven you're not that far.
things get away from me and go so bad,
I'm not helpless, I'm just sad.
so I turn to you with what I have left,
I turn to you in faith I know your ears aren't deaf.
Lord fix what you will and give me the strength to go on
I'll continue to sing a heavenly song.
you are Lord of my life and I love you so,
you never fail to let your love show.

A SONG ON MY LIPS

A song on my lips, your words at my fingertips,
I believe your words, warnings, songs and quips.
to walk in your grace puts a smile on my face,
to walk in your grace is just the best place.
when I'm out of step I don't see the light,
but when in your grace the light shines so bright.
I speak of your grace and works of love,
the kind that only comes from heaven above.
I talk of happiness and peace that fill me inside,
of how all my transgressions you set aside.
there is so much to say when it comes to you,
from all of your love to the things you do.

I FEEL FOR THOSE WHO DON'T KNOW

I feel so bad for those who don't know,
what Christians know about how God's love will show.
They miss out on an unconditional love,
the kind that comes from God above.
they miss out on a friend to turn to no matter what,
on a door that is open and never shut.
there is a comfort in depending on advice always good,
that is for our benefit so things turn out as they should
they miss out on a love that's tender and true,
on being accepted for all that is you.
things aren't always easy but faith will get you through
you have a loving God to show you the way through.
they miss the provider who always knows what you need
it's for all he gave his life and would bleed.
there is still so much more that a non-believer will miss,
but there is so much to gain, I can promise this.

CAN WE TALK?

Lord can we talk? I've had a hard day,
devoured by the world, I feel I've lost my way.
I lost my temper, cursed using your name,
I struck out with my fist rather than assume any blame.
I consulted a medium, it was the wrong thing to do,
showing me my future is up to you.
I coveted my friend's wife because she was there,
I took advantage of his absence, it wasn't fair.
I lied about my friend just to get my own way,
I played the game the world plays.
in my dishonest dealing i swore on your name all was true,
now I'm feeling horrible and don't know what to do.
So Lord I ask your forgiveness and to fix all I did,
I did horrible things, I did the devil's bid.
I ask one other thing if I may of you,
in the future please control the bad things i could do.

LITTLE CREATURES

Even little creatures God gave to this earth,
It's been this way since earth's birth.
The mouse, squirrels and the rabbit too,
dogs, monkeys even the kangaroo.
God loves and cares for all he made,
even oceans and forests and a single grass blade
God love and cares for much more by far,
he loves each of us the way we are.
he has given us the land on which to roam,
but this earth is not our home.
so when you look around be kind to our friends,
they were put here to remain until the earth ends

GOD'S WAY

God, you never promised I'd be rich or have an easy life
You only promised to do for me what is right

Your version and mine may not agree
But I believe the promises you gave to me

Because I've experienced your awesome love
I have faith in you from up above

So as I face trials and tribulations
I'm grateful when I see your revelations

I believe your promise with faith in my heart
I know you're with me and will never part

TAKE ME

Dear Lord I am willing, I give you my life
It's full of problems and full of strife
I have your promise, you'll fix it all
You can make the mighty of the small

I want to trust you, have better than I had
I've done some sinning, done some things bad
I come to you now to transform me
To live as an example all can see

Take me now Lord, my mind and heart
On my own I don't know where to start
I praise you Lord for the changes you'll make
Save me now for goodness sake

ANEW

Come to God, let the rescue begin
He will mend all from within
He's waiting to give you all the love you desire
Don't be afraid, He'll walk with you through fire

God will carry you when you can't go on
He has great love for you from beyond
Just ask, it's given, all past sorrow is gone
Awake to the promise in a new dawn

You don't have to wait, it's there for you now
Just reach out your hand He'll show you how

GIRL OF MY PAST

Dear girl I was in the past
I tell you there is love that will last
Your sorrows, your troubles, your broken pieces
There is a time and place where this all ceases

Come to God, find the place you've dreamed of
It's God's perfect, caring love from above
It's scary to pick up and leave everything you know
But give Him a chance, God's love will show

What's ahead is better than you have known
You will never again walk alone
Blessings waiting, a love not forsaking
It is all there just for the taking

So come, come to the Lord he is waiting
His hand is there, it is not fading

Oh come to the Lord he is waiting!

Blessed

Made in the USA
Middletown, DE
06 March 2023